Serpents and Werewolves

For Gowan, Mirren, and Colin,
the three most magical people in my life!

Darby Creek
A division of Lerner Publishing Group, Inc.
241 First Avenue North
Minneapolis, MN 55401 USA

For reading levels and more information, look up this title at
www.lernerbooks.com.

Main body text set in Sabon LT Std 13/19.
Typeface provided by Adobe Systems.

Library of Congress Cataloging-in-Publication Data

Names: Don, Lari, author. | Greenwood, Francesca, illustrator.
Title: Serpents and werewolves : stories of shape-shifters from around the
   world / by Lari Don ; illustrations by Francesca Greenwood.
Description: Minneapolis : Darby Creek, 2016. | Series: World of stories |
   Audience: Age: 7–12. | Audience: Grade 4 to 6.
Identifiers: LCCN 2015046855 (print) | LCCN 2016006993 (ebook) |
   ISBN 9781512413212 (lb : alk. paper) | ISBN 9781512413434 (pb :
   alk. paper) | ISBN 9781512413441 (eb pdf)
Subjects: LCSH: Shapeshifting—Juvenile literature.
Classification: LCC GR825 .D66 2016 (print) | LCC GR825 (ebook) |
   DDC 398.2—dc23

LC record available at http://lccn.loc.gov/2015046855

Manufactured in the United States of America
1-39780-21318-3/2/2016

WORLD of STORIES

Serpents and Werewolves

STORIES OF SHAPE-SHIFTERS FROM AROUND THE WORLD

LARI DON

Illustrated by
Francesca Greenwood

darbycreek
MINNEAPOLIS

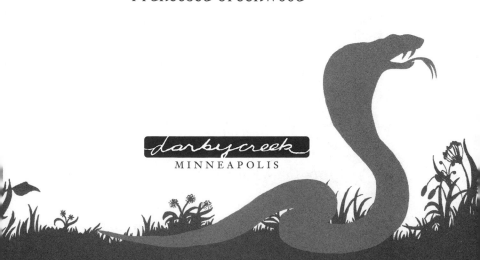

Contents

The Snake Prince
Punjabi Folktale

Snakes can hide in the most unlikely places.

One hot morning, an old woman carried her clay pot down to the river. She stood the pot on the riverbank while she washed her hands and face. When she lifted the pot to fill it with water, she saw a snake coiled up inside.

A small, brightly colored snake.

It was beautiful, but she knew that such

bright colors usually meant deadly poison. The snake hissed at her and stuck out its forked tongue. She threw her veil over the top of the pot and backed away.

But it was her only clay pot. She couldn't afford to buy another. She had to get rid of the snake. She took a deep breath and used a stick to lift the veil.

The snake had vanished.

Inside the pot now was a beautiful necklace, made of gleaming gold and bright jewels, shaped like a snake with its tail in its mouth.

The old woman gasped. She'd never seen anything so beautiful (except possibly the snake, with its vivid, jewel-colored scales) and she'd certainly never seen anything so valuable.

She picked up the pot, with the necklace rattling inside, and she ran to the king's palace. She showed the serpent necklace to the king and queen and told them the story of the

snake in the pot, which they laughed at kindly. They offered her many coins for the necklace. She accepted because coins to buy food were more use to her than fancy jewelry.

The king and queen laid the necklace in a wooden box in their room for the queen to wear on a special occasion.

And a special occasion arrived the next day. The king and queen were invited to a feast in the neighboring kingdom to celebrate the birth of a baby princess. The queen tried to smile when she read the invitation. She had no children of her own, and while she was pleased for the neighboring queen, she was sad too.

"Cheer up," said the king, "this is a chance to wear that beautiful serpent necklace."

They went to the bedroom and opened the wooden box.

The necklace had vanished.

Inside the box now was a baby boy, waving his arms and gurgling.

A perfect, healthy, smiling baby boy.

The queen picked up the baby and hugged him. "This is a gift to us. A child, at last!"

So they raised the boy as their own, as the prince of their kingdom. When he was eighteen, he was betrothed to the princess next door.

But rumors of his unusual arrival, whispered stories of clay pots and snakes and necklaces, had spread from his city to the neighboring kingdom. The princess heard people mutter that she was going to marry a snake prince.

At the feast to celebrate their betrothal, the princess whispered to the prince, "Is it true that you're really a snake?"

He refused to answer.

She asked again, "Are you really a snake? Tell me the truth or I'll refuse to marry you."

He answered, "You will regret it if I tell you the truth."

"We will both regret it if you don't. I can't marry a man who keeps secrets from me."

So they left the feast and sat on the veranda, overlooking the river.

The prince sighed. "As a tiny child, I was enchanted by the Queen of the . . . erm . . . slithering things to be . . . umm . . . a thing

with scales. But I was granted the right to be human until someone asked me that very question. Until someone forced me to utter the word . . ."

"What word? What were you turned into? Who enchanted you? Tell me everything!"

"I was enchanted by the Queen of the Snakes . . ."

As soon as he said the word *snakes,* the young man vanished.

And the princess was sitting on the veranda beside a snake. A long, smooth, beautifully colored snake. Its head drooped sadly onto the ground, then it slid away into the darkness.

The princess sighed. She knew his secret, but now she had lost him forever.

Unless she could persuade the Queen of the Snakes to give him back.

The next morning the princess spoke to the men who charmed snakes in the marketplace. She spoke to the king and queen about the day they found their son. She spoke to the old woman, now ancient and happy in her comfortable home.

The princess came up with a plan. She rented a house by the river. At sunset, she filled four wide bowls with warm milk and sugar and laid those four bowls in the four corners of her bedroom. She sat cross-legged in the middle of the room, and she waited.

She heard a gentle hissing. Then snakes came in through the windows and the door and up through holes in the floor. Big snakes and little snakes, long snakes and short snakes, snakes as dark as night and snakes as bright as sunlight.

The snakes slithered around the princess and the snakes slithered over the princess.

The princess sat still and quiet and respectful.

The snakes slithered toward the bowls of sweet milk. But they didn't drink. They were all waiting for someone. For something.

Then the Queen of the Snakes arrived.

The princess stood up as a huge snake approached the doorway, slipping and sliding along the ground, long and muscular and sinuous, with dark green scales. The huge

 12

snake rose up, her hooded head higher than the princess.

The princess said, "Greetings, Queen of the Snakes."

The Queen of the Snakes opened her huge jaws, showed her sharp fangs, and spoke. "You have gifts for me."

"I have the drink that snakes love the most. I will put four bowls out for you and your people every night of my life if you will give the prince back his human form."

"You dare to bargain with me?" The Queen of the Snakes slithered forward. Her head rose higher. Her eyes and fangs swayed above the princess's head.

The princess stood firm. "Yes. You have something that I want. Give him to me, and I will give you and your followers sweet milk every night."

The Queen of the Snakes hissed and flicked her tongue.

The princess stood firm.

The Queen of the Snakes jerked her head forward and jabbed her fangs into the air just by the princess's left shoulder.

The princess stood firm.

The Queen of the Snakes jerked her head forward and jabbed her fangs into the air just by the princess's right shoulder.

The princess stood firm.

The Queen of the Snakes nodded. "We will drink and you will have your prince."

She lowered her head delicately to the floor and moved to the largest bowl of milk. She drank, then the other snakes drank, then they left the room slowly, with the dry, smooth noise of scales on wood.

But one snake, with a pattern of bright gems along its back, remained in the middle of the room.

That snake writhed and wriggled and squirmed out of its bright skin. And the prince stood up.

He thanked the princess for freeing him from the Queen of the Snakes, then he smiled.

"So, are we going to entertain a houseful of snakes every night of our lives?"

The princess laughed. "No; we'll put the bowls of milk in the garden from now on!"

And they lived in contentment for many years, with only a few small secrets inside their palace and many fat snakes outside.

The First Werewolves
Greek myth

The feet of the gods walked the earth long before the paws of werewolves ran here.

Many years ago, Zeus came to Earth disguised as a traveler. He walked the lands and islands of Greece to see how people lived.

After many miles, he arrived at the castle of King Lycaon. The people in the villages around recognized a strange power in Zeus. The sparking light in his eyes perhaps, or the

rolling note in his voice. They bowed before him and offered him their best food and drink.

He smiled at them and walked up to the castle. He wanted to meet King Lycaon and his sons because he'd heard rumors of their cruelty.

The king heard the praise songs of the people below. From high on the walls of his castle, he looked down and saw the traveler approach his gate, dusty and sweaty, with old-fashioned clothes and boots. Yet he could hear the people call this wretch a god . . .

Lycaon refused to believe this man was better than him. "He is not a god," Lycaon said to his three oldest sons. "He is not above us. And we will prove it."

So they invited the traveler in and asked him to wait by the fire while they prepared him a feast.

Down in the kitchen, the king summoned his youngest son, Nyctimus. Lycaon told the boy to stand beside the largest pot in the kitchen. Then Lycaon cut his son's throat, sliced him up, and dropped the flesh into the pot. Lycaon and his three remaining sons added wine,

herbs, and spices to the meat and boiled up a fragrant stew.

"Let's see if that smelly traveler can work out what *this* is," said Lycaon.

They carried the stew up to the feasting hall, sat the traveler at the table, and placed a bowl of stew in front of him.

The traveler hesitated. He sniffed the stew and frowned.

The three sons filled bowls for themselves and took big spoonfuls. "Yum, delicious, very filling," they said.

So the traveler took a bit of meat and put it to his lips.

Then he roared with anger. He stood, lifted the table into the air, and tipped it over. Bowls and spoons clattered to the floor; stew spilled everywhere.

"HOW DARE YOU? How dare you test a god this way? How dare you treat a guest this way? And how dare you, how *dare* you eat the flesh of your own kind?"

As the god roared, his eyes flashed lightning and his voice boomed with thunder.

Lycaon recognized Zeus. The king fell to the ground and groveled. "We only wished to test your power so that you could reveal your greatness to us, oh great powerful one."

"HOW DARE YOU?" Zeus thundered again.

Lycaon and his sons ran . . .

They had tested the god, they had discovered his power, and now they were terrified. So they ran out of the castle, past the village and toward the hills.

But as they ran, they tripped and stumbled and started to run on four legs, not two. Their fine clothes became ragged and gray and hairy and the fabric stuck to their skin like fur.

They screamed in terror until their screams became howls.

And finally, they were wolves, running into the wilderness, running from the people who would always fear them and hunt them. They would never eat hot meat in a warm castle again.

Zeus waved his hand over the lumps of stew and pools of gravy on the floor. The

 19

boy Nyctimus stood, brushing herbs from his shoulders and spices from his hands. Zeus lifted him onto the throne.

Then Zeus rose up to Olympus to eat ambrosia for his supper and to tell his family about the goodness and evil he'd found as he walked the earth.

Lycaon and his oldest sons ran through the hills as the first-ever pack of werewolves. Cold and hungry and forever hunted by men.

They howled their pain and sorrow and anger. They howled their unhappiness to the gods in the sky every night. But Zeus didn't listen because gods rarely do.

Catching Loki
Norse myth

Loki, the Viking god of mischief, was on the run.

One of his tricks had gone too far, and he was hiding from the Viking gods so they wouldn't punish him for tricking blind Hodur into killing his own brother, Baldur.

Loki was sure the gods wouldn't find him because Loki knew he was smarter than all the other gods put together.

First he climbed high into the mountains.

Then he built himself a house with four doors facing north, east, south, and west so he could see his pursuers approaching from any direction.

Then he worked out his escape route.

If they found him, Loki wouldn't have to run away on his two human legs. Loki was a shape-shifter. He could become a falcon or a fly or a horse. This time he thought he'd become a fish.

He'd built his house by a narrow river just below a waterfall, and he decided that if the gods approached, he would turn into a fish and leap into the water.

So Loki hid in his four-doored house by his fast, cold river. And the gods didn't find him.

But do you know how boring it is playing hide and seek if no one finds you? Loki was used to tricks and mischief and games and quests, so he became *very* bored hiding in his four-doored house, high and lonely in the mountains.

He started to chat to himself. "None of

those thick-headed warrior gods will be able to catch me. The only god who would ever be able to catch me is myself.

"If I was chasing me, how would I catch me?"

Loki sat by the fire in the center of his four-doored house, glancing north, east, south, and west. He fiddled with a bit of string. And he wondered, if he wanted to catch a fish in the river, what would he use?

He would need something that would let water through but not let a fish through. Something light but strong. Something flexible. Loki fiddled with the string. He imagined catching a fish. He knotted, he twisted, and he invented . . .

He invented a net. The very first fishing net.

He looked at it and laughed. "A net. That's the only thing that could catch me! And those muscle-bound idiots couldn't invent this. They need me to do their thinking for them. I will always be safe from them because I will always be smarter than them."

Then he saw them. Through the east door, he saw the gods approach. Big, tall gods with axes, hammers, spears, swords, and daggers.

Loki wasn't scared. He knew his brains were a match for their weapons.

So he stepped to the north door, which led to the river and the waterfall.

Then he glanced back and saw the fishing net on the floor. "I can't leave that for them." So he kicked the net toward the fire, ran out the door, and dove into the river, changing into a salmon as he dove.

Loki hid under the water, hoping to return to his four-doored house once the search party moved on.

The gods stood outside the house.

"Four doors," said Thor, god of thunder. "That's clever. That has the smell of Loki."

The gods stepped inside the house.

"He's not here," said Tir, god of war. "He saw us coming and fled. Tricksy coward. We'll have to keep searching."

But Honir, the god of silence, was pointing at the fire.

There were dark marks on the floor near the fire. A pattern of ash, a latticework of burned lines and knots.

The gods stared at it.

"What is it?"

"Why would he make that?"

"Why would he *burn* that?"

The god of silence pointed at the river.

The gods smiled.

"What would that pattern catch?" said Thor.

"That might catch a fish . . ." said Tir.

So they sat down, they copied the pattern on the floor, and they made the second fishing net.

They took it outside, they stretched it across the river, then Thor and Tir walked slowly up the riverbanks, pulling the net between them, driving any fish in the river toward the waterfall.

As the gods and their net forced Loki upriver, toward the trap of the high, rocky fall, Loki realized he had no option but to reveal himself. He leaped out of the

water, hoping to jump over the net and swim away.

But Thor's fast hand grabbed the fish as he leaped. Thor slammed the fish down on the bank so hard that Loki became man-shaped again, then bound Loki so tightly that the shape-shifter couldn't shift again.

And Loki was taken back to Odin to face justice. Loki, the trickster god, finally caught in a net he'd invented himself. Finally caught by his own cleverness.

The Ashkelon Witches
Jewish Folktale

Once there was a coven of eighty witches who lived in a cave above the town of Ashkelon and enjoyed tormenting the people of the town.

They often caused fires to blow out and cows to run dry of milk. Then one day, they turned a whole family into winged creatures. The father and sons turned into birds, the mother and daughters turned into butterflies, and the new baby turned into a caterpillar.

The local rabbi, Rabbi Shimon ben Shetah, decided the witches had gone too far and it was time to get rid of them.

He waited for a day of heavy rain because in his wisdom he knew that witches are terrified of rain. He called seventy-nine of his students to him. He told each student to fetch two robes and a large pot, then to wear one robe, to fold the other, and to place it in the pot.

The rabbi and his students walked up the hill to the cave, balancing the pots upside down on their heads, keeping the second robes dry in the rain. Just inside the entrance to the cave, they changed into their dry robes and rolled the pots containing the wet robes out of sight down the hill.

Then the rabbi called, "Witches, come out to dance with me and my fine young students!"

The witches replied from the depths of the cave. "We can't come out today. It's raining."

"But our robes are dry!" said the rabbi.

"How could we be standing here completely dry in our best robes if it was raining? Here, touch my robe."

Hands reached out of the darkness: pale hands and dark hands, old wrinkled hands and young smooth hands, hands with long claws and hands with bitten-down nails.

The hands stroked the rabbi's dry robe.

There was a moment's silence. The students held their breath.

"It's not raining!" the witches yelled. "If it's not raining, we can dance!"

"We'll wait for you outside, ladies." The rabbi led his students out of the cave onto the hillside.

As the witches tidied their hair and put on their dancing shoes, they whispered and giggled. "When we're tired of dancing with that foolish rabbi and his boys, let's turn them into beetles!"

"Or toads!"

"Or fleas!"

Still laughing, the witches stepped out into the rain.

The moment the falling water hit them, they lost all their magic.

As the rabbi and his students watched, each witch was transformed.

Those who had set spells to make fires die became flames, to be blown away as ash on the wind.

Those who had set spells to make the cows run dry became blades of grass, to be eaten by the animals of the hill.

And those who had set spells to turn the family into winged creatures became worms on the ground, to be pecked up by the early birds of the morning.

When the rabbi and his students returned, soaking wet, to Ashkelon, they discovered that the transformed family had changed from birds and butterflies back into people.

But the baby was screaming angrily because she'd enjoyed being a wriggly caterpillar!

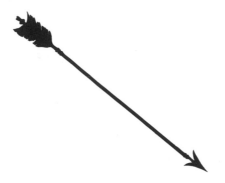

Turnskin
Breton Folktale

This story starts where most stories end: *and they lived happily ever after* . . .

Because this story starts with a tall, dark, handsome young lord meeting and marrying a delicate, golden, city girl, then taking her home to his castle in Brittany, where they both hoped to live happily ever after.

But what happens *after* happily ever after?

The lord and his lady were happy for a month. Then the lord, Bisclavret, went missing

for three days. He simply vanished into the thick forest around his castle.

When he came back, he refused to tell his new wife where he'd been and he expected their happy ever after to continue. But she was confused and worried.

The same thing happened the next month and the month after. Every month, Bisclavret was absent for a few days.

She demanded answers. "Where do you go? What do you do? Who are you *with*?"

But every time she asked, he changed the subject or made a joke.

He continued to disappear every month for three or four days. Leaving his new young wife in charge of the castle, the lands, the staff, and the guards and refusing to answer her questions when he returned.

Eventually she said, "Bisclavret, we can't have a happily ever after unless you share your secrets with me. Tell me where you go and what you do. If you don't, I'll know you don't love me after all."

Bisclavret stopped joking and evading. He

sighed and said he was afraid that if he told her, she would no longer love him. His new wife smiled and held his hand and promised that whatever he said she would still love him.

So he told her his secret.

"I am a turnskin," he said. "My skin is human on the outside but on the inside, my skin is covered with dark gray hair. On the inside, I wear wolfskin. When I feel the itch start and the turn approach, I leave my castle and my people and I go into the forest so I can't hurt anyone."

His wife let go of his hand and wrapped her arms around her chest. "You become a wolf?"

"Yes. I become a wolf. I knew you would be shocked. I knew you would stop loving me."

"But I don't understand. How do you eat, where do you sleep . . . ? If I can understand, if you tell me everything, I'm sure I will still love you." She took his hand again, her fingers trembling.

Bisclavret told her almost everything. How he lived in the forest, what he hunted, how it felt to run and howl. There was only one thing he didn't tell her.

"I can't tell you where I hide my clothes," he said when she asked. "That's the one thing a turnskin has to keep secret because we need to find and wear our own clothes to turn human again."

Bisclavret's wife smiled and said she understood. And they seemed to live happily ever after for a few more weeks.

But she didn't like her husband having even one secret, so when he left the castle the next month, she followed him. He wasn't hard to follow in his bright red cloak.

She followed him from the castle to the edge of the forest and through the forest to a small clearing. She hid behind a bush and watched as he took off his red cloak, his white shirt, his long brown leather boots, and his gray breeches. She watched as he folded his clothes, then lifted a stone and hid the clothes in a hole underneath.

Then she watched as he changed. He crouched to the ground and his spine arched. His arms stretched and his legs shrank to become four limbs the same length. His fingers clenched into paws and his nails curved into claws. His nose and chin melted together, then jutted out into a long snout with yellow fangs.

She watched as his skin rippled, then turned so he was covered in dark gray fur.

She watched as he became a wolf.

Then she watched as the wolf lifted his snout, sniffed the air, and slowly turned his head toward the bush she was hiding behind.

She felt her own skin ripple, a tiny cold shiver of fear across her neck and shoulders. Then the wolf turned away and trotted off into the forest.

The new wife couldn't move. She had understood the idea of her husband becoming a wolf when they'd talked. But she'd not expected the reality of watching her handsome husband become a beast and of fearing that the beast would attack her.

She didn't want to be married to him anymore.

She couldn't have a happily ever after with an animal. She never wanted to see him again.

So she stood, she walked to the stone, she kicked it over, she picked up the clothes, and she walked away.

Carrying the red cloak wrapped around the rest of the clothes, she walked through the forest toward the castle, up the wide steps, and through the arched doorway. She washed the clothes and dried them. She hung the cloak behind the door. She folded the shirt and breeches and put them in a drawer. She polished the boots.

Then she took control of the castle just as she had every time her husband was absent. But this time, she had a plan.

She ordered the men to cut down the trees for a quarter of a mile around the castle so the land was bare and anything crossing the land could be easily seen. She gave each man a bow and a quiver full of arrows, then sent them to the top of the towers and battlements and ordered them to shoot any animal that left the forest.

Then she relaxed, sure she would never see Lord Bisclavret again, as a wolf or a man.

In the forest, the turnskin spent three days as a wolf, hunting and running and sleeping under the trees. Then when his skin itched and he knew it was time to turn back to a man, he returned to the clearing. But the stone was on its side, the hole was empty, and his clothes were gone.

Bisclavret knew that to become a man again, he must find clothes. He had plenty of clothes in his castle so he went toward the edge of the forest, which was much nearer than he expected. He stepped out into the bare land between the trees and the castle, and suddenly—THUMP—an arrow hit the earth beside him.

He ran back into the forest, turned to look at the castle and saw men, his own men, aiming arrows at him.

So he waited until night and tried again. But the guards had put burning torches into

the ground around the castle, and though the wolf got a little nearer, the arrows still flew out of the dark at him, and he had to run back to the safety of the trees.

Bisclavret realized he couldn't reach the castle and find his own clothes. So he ran in the other direction until he found a woodsman's cottage on the other side of the forest. He stole a shirt from the washing line and struggled his front legs into the sleeves. But he didn't turn into a man because these weren't his own clothes and they had no power to turn him back.

The turnskin gave up.

He stayed a wolf because he had no choice, and anyway he enjoyed being a wolf. He enjoyed the chase when he hunted deer, he enjoyed the hot bloody meat, he enjoyed the strength and speed of his muscles, he enjoyed the weight and warmth of his soft fur, and he enjoyed the world of scents around him.

But after weeks of living as a lone wolf, he began to miss the things that made him a man. He missed bread and cheese and baths.

He missed music and stories and friendship. He missed his wife and his happily ever after.

So he tried to reach his own clothes again. But the land around the castle was still bare ("Who ordered the trees cut down?" he wondered). The archers were still on the battlements ("Who put them there?" he wondered). And there was still no way to get to his own clothes ("Who took my clothes from the forest?" he wondered).

As he prowled alone through the forest, he heard a horn. A shrill hunting horn echoing through the trees. All wild animals are afraid of the hunt, but the turnskin ran toward the sound of the horn, toward the baying dogs, drumming hooves, and shouting men.

Then he leaped out right in front of the hunt.

The lead huntsman called, "Halloo! A wolf! A wolfskin cloak for the man who brings it down!"

So the wolf ran.

But not at top speed. He ran just fast enough to keep ahead of the dogs, the horses,

and the huntsmen's spears. He ran through the trees but not into the darkest and thickest parts of the forest. He let the hunt keep him in sight.

He led the hunt to the edge of the forest.

Then the wolf ran out across the bare land. The archers on the castle walls raised their bows and aimed their arrows.

The hunt crashed out of the trees and the lead huntsman yelled, "NO! Don't shoot! The wolf is ours. Don't shoot our prey."

The archers lowered their bows and watched the chase. They watched the wolf dash across the cleared land, followed by the dogs, the horses, and the men with spears.

Now the wolf *was* running as fast as possible. He sprinted toward the castle with the dogs at his heels.

Chased by the hunt and protected by the hunt.

At the bottom of the steps, where a wild animal would turn and face its foe, the wolf ran up the steps like a man late for a feast. He pushed through the arched wooden doors

and into the castle.

The wolf slid and clattered on the stone floor. He saw his cloaks hanging behind the door. Including his red cloak, which he'd hidden in the forest.

Then he heard a gasp and turned around to see his wife, her face pale and her hands trembling.

Suddenly Bisclavret knew who had taken his clothes, who had cleared the land, and who had ordered the archers to shoot him.

He leaped at his wife, snarling.

He snapped his teeth, just grazing the very tip of her nose.

Then he heard the huntsmen running up the steps. He turned his back on his wife and used his teeth to haul down the cloak.

The huntsmen shoved the door wide open. And they saw . . .

. . . the lord, Bisclavret, tall and dark and handsome, wrapped from throat to heels in a rich red cloak.

"What are you doing, barging into my castle?"

"Sorry, sire. We thought we saw a wolf run in here."

"A wolf? In a castle? Don't be ridiculous."

The hunters apologized, left the castle, and headed back to the forest to find easier prey.

Bisclavret turned to ask his new wife why she had betrayed him, what had happened to her promise to love him whatever his secret, and whether they could still find their happily ever after together.

But she had gone.

He searched the house for her until finally, glancing out of a window, he saw her. Running across the bare land toward the edge of the forest.

He didn't chase her. He let her go.

And so, once upon a time, a girl who had been bitten by a werewolf ran into the forest . . . which might be the start of a new story.

The Swallow's Search
Egyptian myth

A family full of gods is not always a happy family.

The Egyptian god Set was jealous of his older brother, Osiris, because Osiris was loved by the people and because Osiris had a beautiful and powerful wife, Isis.

So Set came up with a plan to get rid of Osiris. He invited Osiris and all his men to a party at his riverside palace and provided a wonderful feast with lots of bread and beer.

At the end of the meal, when everyone was full and happy, Set announced that he had a splendid gift for one of his guests but he didn't yet know who it was for.

He brought out a gorgeous wooden chest, carved and fragranced and inlaid with gems, and said it was a gift for the person who fit most neatly inside.

All his guests tried. But everyone was too fat or too thin or too short or too tall.

Everyone apart from Osiris.

Osiris fit perfectly. His shoulders spanned the width of the chest, his feet touched the base, and his hair just brushed the top.

It was as if the box had been carved specially for him.

Osiris lay comfortably in the box and laughed. "It seems this pretty box is mine, Set."

Set laughed too. "Yes, brother, it is your box. It is your coffin!"

Set slammed the lid down, nailed it shut and, before Osiris's men could react, Set shoved the chest into the River Nile. As it

floated away into the darkness, Set knew he had finally got rid of Osiris.

Isis soon heard of Set's trick.

First the goddess placed her young son and heir, Horus, on an island. To keep the boy hidden from Set, she cut the island loose from the riverbed and sent it floating across the waters so it was never in the same place twice.

Then Isis began to search for her husband.

She spread her arms, whispered her secret name, and became a bird. She became a swallow.

She flew high above the Nile, searching for her beloved Osiris. At first she was searching for him to rescue him, to free him from that beautiful box and let him breathe fresh air again.

After many days of searching, she knew Osiris couldn't have survived so long without food or water or air. Now Isis was searching for his body to perform the rites that would free his spirit.

She searched and searched, flying along the

length of the Nile, across the vast width of its mouth, even out over the salty sea beyond. But she didn't see the glittering box anywhere. Because the box wasn't on the river.

On the very first day, the box had been swept up against the riverbank where it banged into a tamarind tree. The tree, enchanted by the beauty of the box, had wrapped itself around Osiris's coffin and engulfed the box in its broad trunk.

The box and the body were hidden inside the tree.

Then the tree was chopped down, carried to a local king's palace, and turned into a pillar to hold up the roof.

So no matter how fast and far she flew, Isis would never find the box on the river.

Then she heard rumors, as birds do, about a marvelous new pillar, of thrumming power and amazing beauty, so she flew to the king's palace to see this pillar. She transformed back into the shape of a woman and offered her services to the queen as the baby Prince's nurse.

As Isis cared for the boy and became fond of him, she wondered why she was so drawn to the wooden pillar.

One night, the queen heard odd noises from the baby's room. She pushed the door open to see . . .

. . . her baby boy burning in the center of a fire!

Her child was lying in the middle of blazing flames. His nurse was nowhere to be seen. There was a swallow swooping around the pillar in the center of the room.

The queen screamed and rushed forward to pull her son from the flames. She burned her hands pulling him out.

But the baby was smiling and unharmed.

The swallow hovered in midair, then grew and stretched and became the boy's nurse.

"Foolish woman," said the nurse to the queen. "I was burning the mortality off your son; I was turning him into a god. You have broken the spell. He will never be a god now."

The queen sobbed and the baby giggled.

"However, I will bless him before I leave," said Isis, "if you will have your servants cut this pillar open, because I believe there is something precious inside."

The baby received one last hug from his nurse as the pillar was sawn open and the beautiful chest fell out.

Isis arranged a barge to carry the box and the body toward the island where their son Horus waited. But on the journey home, while she slept one night, Set passed by on the riverbank and caught sight of the box glinting in the moonlight.

He didn't want Osiris's powerful spirit to rise free so he crept onto the barge, opened the box, and chopped the body into fourteen pieces. Then he scattered those fourteen pieces over the river and the desert beyond.

When Isis woke and found the box broken open and empty, she transformed into a bird again to search for all the pieces of Osiris. She flew over every inch of Egypt and found thirteen of the fourteen pieces. When she finally realized that the fourteenth piece was

lost forever, she filled the gap with gold and made Osiris whole.

She bound all the pieces of her husband together with linen strips and she spoke the rites. As she whispered goodbye to Osiris, his spirit floated free, down to the Duat where all the spirits go.

In the Duat, Osiris ruled as King of the Dead, while Set ruled above, until Isis and Osiris's son Horus was grown and could defeat Set to restore balance to the world.

Set was defeated thousands of years ago, but even now, Isis occasionally turns into a bird and flies high and far over Egypt, hoping to find that very last piece of Osiris.

The Frog, the Flies, and the Frying Pan
Scottish Folktale

Once upon a time, on the mossy, heathery moors of Scotland, a mother and her daughter lived in a small cottage.

One day, the mother asked, "Would you like oatcakes for tea?"

"Yes, that would be lovely," said the girl.

So the mother fetched a couple of handfuls of oatmeal and a pinch of salt, then realized

there was no fresh water in the house. "The best water for baking is the pure, clear water in the Well at the End of the World." She handed a big jug to her daughter. "If you want oatcakes for tea, fill that jug from the Well at the End of the World, please."

The end of the world sounds like a long way away but Scotland is on the northern edge of Europe, and the end of the world is often just over the horizon.

So the girl faced a long walk but not as long as an expedition or a quest. She spent the morning striding along, swinging the empty jug with every step.

When she reached the white stone well, she sat on the edge and looked in.

The well was empty. The Well at the End of the World was dry.

The girl sighed. "I've walked all the way to the end of the world. Now I'll have to walk all the way home again with an empty jug and there won't be oatcakes for tea."

"Oatcakes!" said a soggy voice. "I love oatcakes."

A frog jumped onto the edge of the well.

A shiny frog, with a yellow belly, a green back, and a long tongue, jumped up right beside the girl. But this frog was shiny like slime rather than polished jewelry. It was green like poison rather than leaves. It was yellow like mustard rather than daffodils. And its long tongue was black and sticky.

The girl stood quickly and stepped away from the frog.

"I love oatcakes," the frog said again.

"There won't be any oatcakes without water," she said.

The frog smiled a gummy wide-mouthed smile. "I can bring the water back to the well, if you make me a couple of promises."

The girl looked at the frog, at the empty well and her empty jug, then back at the frog. The frog flicked its tongue out and caught a fly. Then ate it.

"Yuck," said the girl.

The frog said, "If you want water, you must promise to let me into your house when I knock on the door tonight, and you must promise to

let me sit on your lap and eat oatcakes from your plate."

The girl took another step back and watched the frog flicking out its tongue.

She didn't want to let the frog into her house, or onto her knee, or at her oatcakes. But she thought, *This frog doesn't know where I live and it can't possibly hop as fast as I walk, so I can safely make those promises and never see this frog again.*

So she said, "Yes, I promise that if you knock on my door tonight, I'll let you in, let you sit on my knee, and let you eat my oatcakes. But first, you have to find me water."

The frog hopped around the well three times, and as he completed his third circle, the well flooded with pure clean water.

The girl dipped her jug in and filled it to the brim. Then she walked off, swinging the heavy jug.

The frog called after her, "Remember your promise!"

She turned around and

saw the frog, with a fly half in and half out of its mouth, one tiny clear wing flapping feebly by the frog's cheek. The frog crunched and the wing drooped.

The girl made a face. "Oh yuck! I mean, oh yes; I'll remember." She walked off, swinging the jug, drops of water flying out at every step. Leaving a trail of dark dots on the ground behind her.

She walked all the way home from the end of the world.

She helped her mother mix the oats and water, roll and cut the oatcakes, and bake them in the oven. When the oatcakes were still warm, they set the table with soft butter, crumbly cheese, and hot broth.

As they sat down to eat, there was a knock at the door. A soft, squelchy knock. The girl put her head in her hands.

Her mother said, "Answer the door, please."

"Erm . . . no. I really don't want to. Let's have a quiet evening, just the two of us."

There was another soft knock.

"Answer the door, my girl."

"I can't; my legs are stiff after that long walk."

"Nonsense. Answer the door, now."

"No, I won't!"

"Then I will!" Her mother stood and walked toward the door. "Who's there?"

"It's me, the frog your daughter promised to let in if I knocked on the door tonight."

The mother looked at the girl. "You made a promise? To a frog?"

"Erm . . . yes."

"Then come here and open this door!"

The girl got up, walked slowly to the door, and opened it. The shiny green frog hopped inside. The girl sighed.

The frog said, "Now let me sit on your lap and eat from your plate."

"No! That would be too gross."

"But you promised!"

"Did you promise?" asked her mother.

"Yes, I suppose I did promise."

"Then keep your promise," her mother said firmly.

So the girl sat down, the frog jumped onto her lap, and she leaned back, making a face,

keeping her hands well away from the frog's glistening skin.

The frog put its front feet on the table and started to eat one of the oatcakes from her plate. It used its long tongue and soft lips, and it dribbled and drooled as it worked the oatcake into soggy lumps, then swallowed them.

The girl leaned back even further, muttering, "Yuck, I'll never be able to eat another oatcake."

Then the frog pulled itself up on the table. "There is one more thing I want you to do for me."

The girl pushed her chair back, stood, and stared at the frog squatting in the middle of the table.

"Just one more thing," the frog said.

The girl had read the right books and heard the right stories, so she said, "No! No way! I am not kissing you! I've seen you eat *flies* with your flicky tongue and there is no way I will ever kiss you. Not for a jug of water. Not for a jug of gold coins. Not for anything. I will never kiss you!"

The frog shrugged. "That's fine. I don't want a kiss. I want you to hit me on the head with an iron pan. I want you to strike me with cold iron."

"You want me to hit you on the head with a pan?" asked the girl.

The frog nodded.

"You want me to hit you *hard* with a pan?"

The frog nodded again.

"Fine. I will happily whack you with a pan."

She picked up a frying pan and lifted it above her own head.

"No!" yelled her mother. "If you hit the frog, you'll squish it!"

"That's the idea!" said the girl as she lifted the pan higher. She brought the pan down as hard as she could. Right on top of the frog's green shiny head.

The frog vanished.

The table smashed.

And standing there, in the midst of the wrecked table, was a young man, tall and elegant in a green satin coat and a yellow velvet waistcoat.

He smiled. "Thank you so much for freeing me from my curse. I was traveling in your land and I met a witch who cursed me to be a frog until a girl let me eat from her plate then struck me with iron. So, thank you."

He knelt down and took the girl's hand. "We must do this the traditional way. You've lifted my curse and returned me to my true form, so would you like to marry me?"

The girl took her hand back gently. "Not really, no. I've seen you eat flies. A fly half out of your mouth, with its wing still fluttering, is not an image I'll ever forget. So, no, I don't want to marry you. But thanks."

The young man sighed with relief and stood. "Then I shall continue my journey and my adventures. And I shall try not to annoy any other witches and get turned into any other animals. Thank you for your help and for the lovely oatcakes."

He bowed to the mother and the daughter, left the cottage, and walked away from the end of the world.

The girl stood at the doorway and called

after him, "If you do annoy another witch and do get turned into another animal, you're welcome to come back here and I'll hit you with the frying pan again!"

I wonder if he ever went back . . . what do you think?

Fooled by Foxes
Japanese Folktale

In Japan, everyone knows what kitsune are but very few people can recognize one.

Kitsune are foxes who can turn into humans or humans who can turn into foxes. Kitsune love to trick people, often persuading men to marry fox-women or leading travelers down dangerous paths.

One day, a dozen young men were drinking tea under the cherry trees in their village and telling kitsune tales. One young man

announced to his friends: "I'd never be fooled by a kitsune!"

His friends laughed. "Scholars and priests and samurai have been fooled by kitsune. Why should you be different?"

The young man grinned and stroked his long, silky black hair, tied in a fashionable topknot. "I can tell the difference between a girl and an animal. I would never be fooled!"

His friends dared him to go to the lonely lands above the village where the local kitsune stories came from, to walk there for a day and a night, and to see if he returned still convinced he'd never be fooled by a fox.

So the young man finished his tea and set off on a long walk.

The land above the village was a mixture of trees and fields, with only a few small farmhouses. The young man walked along the narrow lanes confidently, whistling and pausing to look up at the beautiful mountains.

Suddenly, from behind a slim tree, stepped a slim young woman in a silver kimono and a white headscarf and gloves. She said, "A

traveler! You must be tired and thirsty! Follow me to my family's house and we will give you refreshment and rest."

The young man laughed. "How stupid do you think I am? That tree is far too thin to hide a girl. When you were behind that tree, you were a fox, weren't you? Crouched down waiting for a foolish traveler to walk past?

"There must be pointed ears under that scarf and furry paws under those gloves! I know what you are. You're a fox! You're a kitsune! So I say 'no' to your rest and your refreshment. This is one traveler you won't fool."

The girl blushed. "I'm sorry if I offended you, but I assure you, it was a genuine offer. I'm sorry. I will leave you to continue your journey."

She walked off, heading down the narrow lane. The young man, feeling quite pleased with himself, kept going up the lane.

After he took ten steps, he whirled around. The lane behind him was empty. There was no girl in sight. But he did see a bushy tail vanish into the trees.

"Aha! I was right! She was a kitsune. And she didn't fool me!" He grinned. "But what about all the people around here who aren't as smart as me? I'd better warn them that there's a kitsune about today."

He strode up the path to the nearest farmhouse and knocked on the door.

When the farmer answered, the young man said, "I came to warn you that there's a kitsune about; a tricksy fox-girl. You'd better be on your guard!"

"Goodness me," said the farmer. "You'd better come in and tell us all about it."

The young man went into the small kitchen and saw the farmer's wife sewing by the fire

and a young woman sitting on a stool. The same young woman he'd met on the path.

"That's her! The fox-girl. The kitsune. She's here, ready to trick you all!"

"No, that's my niece, visiting from family far away," said the farmer. "She's not a fox!"

"Yes she is. She absolutely is. I saw her tail; I'll prove it to you." He stepped over to the girl.

"Here are her *ears*!" He pulled off the white scarf. Underneath were delicate human ears.

"Oh. No fox ears. She's a tricky one. But here are her *paws*!" He pulled off the white gloves. Underneath were slim human fingers.

"Oh. No fox paws either. But you're not fooling me, girl. Animals fear fire."

He grabbed the girl's right wrist and dragged her over to the fire. "Let's *burn* the fox out!"

He thrust the girl's hand toward the flames. The girl screamed.

The young man watched her human skin turn red in the heat.

"Oh no! You're not a fox! Oh no!" He pulled the girl from the fireplace, shoved her

into the arms of her aunt, and ran to the other side of the kitchen.

He stood with his back pressed against the wall and stared at the weeping girl.

"I'm sorry. I made a terrible mistake. I'm so sorry. What can I do to make amends? I'll go back to my village and spend all my money on the best creams the healer can offer. We'll heal the burn and your hand will be as good as new. I'm so sorry."

"That's not good enough," said the farmer. "You'll have to do more than that to prove how sorry you are. The priest will know how you can make amends."

The farmer left the kitchen as his wife bandaged the girl's hand, and the young man stood still and silent. Soon the farmer returned with a priest.

"I'm so sorry!" said the young man again. "It was a mistake! What can I do to make amends?"

The priest looked at the girl's hand, then at the young man. "You must let me shave your head. Then for as long as it takes your hair to

grow back, everyone will see the evidence of your terrible mistake and everyone will know your shame."

The young man knelt down. The priest undid his topknot, then shaved off all his hair.

The priest threw handfuls of long black hair into the fire. As the young man breathed the stink of his own hair burning, he fainted and fell face-first onto the tiled floor.

When he woke, he wasn't lying on tiles, he was lying on the earth; he wasn't in a farmhouse, he was in a field. He looked up and saw four foxes running off in the distance. One of the foxes was limping.

He walked back to the village, his shaved head gleaming. And until his hair grew long enough to be tied in a topknot again, everyone could see how he had been fooled not by one fox but by four foxes.

Ceridwen's Potion
Welsh legend

Ceridwen was a powerful sorceress, skilled in many kinds of magic.

Her favorite magic was shape-shifting because she loved to run and eat and sleep as many different animals. She loved the different view of the world she got with different eyes and the different feel of the earth under hooves, or paws, or claws. She loved the challenge of hunting different prey. And she loved learning from different animals while

she lived with them for a day or a week or a month.

But she wanted a human life too, so she became pregnant, to have a human child of her own.

Ceridwen continued shape-shifting while she carried the child in her belly, spending nights as an owl or a badger or a bat and days as a deer or a pigeon or an eel. The constant changes of shape and size may not have been good for her baby because when he was born, he was crooked and crinkled, with odd patches of hair and misshapen feet.

But Ceridwen loved her baby. She called him Afagddu. She would change into a weasel and dance until he giggled or change into a nightingale and sing until he slept.

Though Afagddu wasn't handsome or swift on his limbs, Ceridwen soon realized he was clever. He didn't have the looks to be a prince, nor the strength and balance to be a warrior, but perhaps he could gain respect as a wise man.

So she decided to use her magic to help her

son become happy and successful. She started to brew a potion that would give Afagddu all the wisdom in the world.

It was a complex potion, requiring herbs from all over Wales, picked at very specific times: at midnight in a lightning storm, at sunrise on May Day, at noon on the summer solstice. Ceridwen would need a full year to gather all the ingredients and she could make this potion only once in her life.

She knew that the potion must simmer gently all the time she was collecting ingredients and that the potion must be guarded because the first person to taste it—and only the first person to taste it—would gain all the wisdom in the world.

Ceridwen employed a local boy, Gwion, to stir the potion and keep the fire burning under the pot.

She allowed Afagddu to limp after her as she gathered the herbs, and while they walked she talked to him about plants and their powers.

She gathered goldenrod and sage, dropped them in the pot, and snapped at Gwion, "Keep

stirring, boy, and don't let anyone steal a drop."

She gathered meadowsweet and rosemary, dropped them in the pot, and shouted at Gwion, "Keep stirring, boy, and don't let anyone taste it."

She gathered wormwood and vervain, dropped them in the pot, and yelled at Gwion, "Keep stirring, boy, and guard it with your life."

The potion was almost complete. The final ingredient, to sweeten it, was dew from the white rose at the foot of the tallest mountain. As Ceridwen and Afagddu left early in the morning, she shouted, "Keep that fire bright, boy, and keep stirring!"

Gwion added wood to the fire to make it burn bright, and he stirred. The potion boiled, bubbled, popped, and spat.

One drop of potion flew out of the pot and landed on the back of Gwion's hand, scalding him. Gwion put his hand to his mouth and sucked to cool the pain.

So Gwion was the first person to taste the potion.

Ceridwen returned with Afagddu limping behind her and the white rose in her hands. She saw the light in Gwion's eyes and knew that his mind was alight with all the wisdom in the world.

She screamed, "*You stole my son's wisdom!*" And she leaped toward Gwion.

But Gwion was newly full of wisdom and knowledge and ideas, and he knew that Ceridwen meant to kill him in her anger. So, fast as a heartbeat, he changed into a hare.

The hare bounded off.

Ceridwen changed into a hound and chased the hare.

The hare's long legs were powerful but the hound was just as fast, and unlike Gwion, Ceridwen was used to running as an animal. So the hound began to catch up and the hound's long teeth reached for the hare's spine.

The hare reached the riverbank, then changed, fast as a heartbeat, into a silver

salmon and leaped into the narrow river.

The salmon swam away.

The hound splashed into the river and changed into an otter.

The salmon's tail was powerful and its silver scales sped through the water, but the otter was bigger and started to catch up. The otter's sharp teeth reached for the salmon's tail.

The salmon leaped out of the water and changed, fast as a heartbeat, into a swift. The tiny bird flew up and away.

But the otter scrambled out of the river and changed into a falcon. The falcon flew high above the swift and hovered, then dove, hooked beak and talons ready to tear into the bird's neck and wings.

The swift changed, fast as a heartbeat, into a grain of wheat. The grain fell into a farmyard and lay hidden amongst all the other grains of wheat.

The falcon swooped down and changed into a white hen. The hen began to peck and

swallow all the grains of wheat she could see.

The hen ate the grain that was Gwion. Then the hen became a woman again.

Ceridwen laughed. "That will teach you to steal my magic, my son's future, and wisdom you had no right to. That will be the end of you, Gwion." And she returned to the useless potion and her crooked son.

But it wasn't the end of Gwion. Because it was soon clear to Ceridwen that she was carrying another child in her belly, a child with a fast strong heartbeat.

Nine months later, she gave birth to a baby boy with the light of wisdom still shining in his eyes, and she knew this was Gwion.

She lifted the baby high above her head, intending to throw him to the ground and take her revenge properly this time.

But she couldn't. She'd carried this baby for nine months, just as she'd carried her beloved Afagddu, and she couldn't hurt him.

However her anger at Afagddu's loss meant she couldn't love this new baby. So she wrapped the tiny baby in a blanket, laid

him gently in a coracle, and pushed the small boat into the river. The boat was found by a fisherman, who brought the beautiful shining boy up as his own, calling him Taliesin.

Taliesin became a famous wise man, a bard, and a wizard, respected at all the courts of Europe. Many years later, Taliesin taught all his wisdom to a young magician called Merlin.

Afagddu became a respected healer, using the wisdom he had learned when he followed his mother as she gathered herbs.

Because there is more than one way to gain wisdom.

The Gold Sea
Canadian tribal tale

The people of the nation did not know greed. They knew that wealth was only valuable when it was shared among neighbors.

Then a few local men went to work in the gold mines, learning the greed and speed of the white man's gold rush. When one of the men returned to his village on the bay, he brought greed back with him.

He brought a bag of gold dust and gold

nuggets. He kept the gold to himself. He didn't spend the gold on gifts to give his family. He didn't spend the gold on a feast to feed his neighbors. He boasted of the gold and slept with it every night, curled around it, letting the cold of the gold reach his heart.

Then one night, as he curled up around the cold gold, he became a serpent. A huge, curled serpent with cold, black scales.

The elders said to him, "If you want to become a man again, let go of the gold."

But he hissed at them and wouldn't let go of the gold.

The serpent grew bigger and scalier, and soon he couldn't fit in the house or the village. Soon he was so big and so scaly that he had to slither into the bay.

The serpent lay in the water, curled up around his gold, blocking the entrance to the bay. The people couldn't row their boats out to sea to fish or to trade.

The elders asked him once more to let go of his gold and come back to his people.

He hissed again, a huge hiss which rocked

the sea into tall waves, and he stayed curled up around his gold.

The elders decided that to save the village and release the man from his greed, someone would have to kill the serpent.

But who would do this sad and difficult task?

The people chose the best young man in the village. A careful, polite young man, who shared his fish and furs and helped his mother keep their house clean.

The young man sharpened his knife, washed himself thoroughly, walked to the clifftop in the first light of dawn, stripped off his clothes, and dove into the sea.

He swam up to the serpent and tried to stab his knife into the serpent's flesh. But the serpent's scales were as hard as the rock in a gold mine and the knife just slid off.

All day he swam up and down and around the serpent's body looking for a way between the scales. But there was no gap.

At sunset, he realized he didn't have the energy to swim and search and stab all night.

So as the dying sunlight hit the water, flat and bright from the edge of the sky, the young man shouted to the serpent, "Look, more gold, shining on the tips of the waves!"

The serpent lifted his head to see the sunlight glinting on the waves, to search for more gold to curl up around.

When the serpent moved his head, the young man saw a soft place at his throat, dove toward it, and stabbed his knife in.

The serpent died with gold sunlight in his eyes. His body shrank back to the size of a man and floated away on the shining water.

So the young man opened the bay for boats and released the serpent from his greed. Then the young man swam home, leaving the serpent's gold lying at the bottom of the sea.

The Swan Brothers
Norwegian Folktale

Once there was a duchess who made a very silly wish.

She had twelve sons, all healthy and handsome and happy. But the duchess wasn't happy. She wanted a daughter. She wanted a little girl to dress in silks and ribbons and to bring up as a proper little lady.

One day, the duchess was riding through the forest on her white horse and she saw a

woodcutter's wife gathering sticks, surrounded by a giggling group of pink-cheeked daughters.

As the duchess rode on, she sighed. "I wish I had a little girl. I'd give anything; if only I could have a daughter of my own."

Suddenly a little old lady stood on the path in front of her. "That's a very silly wish. You would actually give *anything* to have a daughter?"

"Oh yes! A perfect little girl, with blonde curls and blue eyes and a sweet smile. That's all I want."

"You have twelve little boys. Aren't they enough?"

"They're almost too much! They're muddy and loud and I can't plait their hair with ribbons. I'd rather have a little girl. I really do wish for a little girl. You're a wrinkly old crone in a forest. Can you grant wishes?"

"I can. But you might not like it if I do."

"Oh please, grant me this one wish. I'd give anything . . ."

"You just have," said the old lady. She turned away to walk into the trees, then she

turned back. "But if your perfect little girl ever wants to undo your silly wish, send her to me."

The duchess went home a bit puzzled but very happy. Nine months later, she gave birth to a perfect baby girl.

The moment the baby was born, the duchess's twelve sons turned into swans and flew away.

The duchess missed her sons, their noise and mud and games, every day. But she did love her little girl.

As the little girl grew up, she heard rumors from the servants about the twelve boys who had lived in the castle before her but she never heard the whole story.

When she was fifteen years old, she asked her mother, "Is it true I had twelve brothers and they were enchanted to become swans the day I was born?"

"Yes, it is, my dear. But don't worry about it. Let me put this velvet ribbon in your hair . . ."

"I don't want another ribbon. I want you to tell me what happened."

Her mother told her, though she carefully

didn't repeat every word the old lady had spoken.

The girl, the sister of those lost brothers, said, "You gave away so many children, just to gain one!"

"But I gained you, my darling. And I wouldn't change that back for the world."

"I would! I can't bear to think of my brothers trapped in birds' bodies, out in all weather, not able to speak or ask for help. I am their sister. I must be able to help them." She held both her mother's hands and looked into her mother's eyes. "What exactly did the old lady say?"

And the duchess, who couldn't refuse her pretty daughter anything, told her exactly what the old lady had said.

So that night, the sister took off her fine clothes and ribbons, put on a plain dress and sensible boots, and went into the forest.

Now the duchess had lost all her children.

The sister walked for many days until she found a cottage with a wrinkled old lady inside. She knocked on the door and asked,

"Did you grant a wish for a perfect little girl to a mother who should have known better?"

"I did. Was she happy with you?"

"Yes, but I doubt my brothers are happy. Can I set them free?"

"Of course. With your bare hands, you must harvest enough nettles to spin and weave and sew twelve shirts for your twelve brothers. When the shirts are ready, the swans will appear, put on the nettle shirts, and change back to boys and men. But while you harvest, spin, weave, and sew, you must not speak. You must stay silent, not utter one word, whatever happens."

The girl thanked her, went deeper into the forest, and began to collect nettles.

She thought the worst thing about her task would be the stinging of the nettles but it wasn't the worst thing. She couldn't sing as she worked. She couldn't mutter rude words when

the leaves stung. She couldn't chat to the birds or butterflies. She had to keep her tongue still and her lips closed. And that was difficult.

For weeks and months, she picked the nettles and stripped the leaves off the stems. Then she spun the sharp fibers into thread and wove the thread into prickly cloth. Finally she started to make shirts.

As she sewed the first shirt, a young king rode by on a hunting expedition.

The king saw the girl, as perfect as her mother had wished for, golden-curled and blue-eyed, sewing quietly under the trees.

He fell in love. Just like that.

He asked her name.

She shook her head.

He asked if he could help with her task.

She shook her head.

He asked if she would join him in the hunt.

She shook her head.

So he sat down beside her and talked. He told her his name, where he lived, how many little brothers and sisters he had, and what his horse's name was. She smiled and he laughed

 84

and she smiled again. But she didn't say a word to him. That was the hardest thing so far. (But not the hardest thing of all. That was still to come.)

He asked her to marry him.

She nodded her head.

So the young king took the beautiful girl, and her spools of thread, her pile of cloth, and the very first nettle shirt, back to his palace.

They were married and she continued her task in the bright rooms of the tower. She was happy, though she couldn't say it out loud.

But the king's mother wasn't happy. The old queen wanted to keep the keys of the kingdom in her own hands; she didn't want to share power, or her son's love, with anyone else.

She kept whispering to her son, "That new wife of yours isn't quite right. She doesn't talk. She insists on weaving and sewing those odd prickly shirts. It's not normal. It's uncanny."

But the young king loved his new queen and he stopped listening to his mother.

So when the new queen had a baby after

 85

a year of marriage, the old queen crept into the tower late at night, stole the child, cut her own thumb, and dribbled her own blood onto the new queen's lips. Then she went into the forest and threw the baby into a pit of snakes and toads.

The next day she called to her son, "It's an outrage! Your creepy, silent wife has eaten her own baby! She must be a witch!"

The young king touched the blood on the lips of his new queen. "Is this true, my love? Is this true? Please speak up in your own defense!"

But she couldn't. She stayed silent and sewed the collar onto the eleventh shirt.

The young king, grieving for his child and goaded by his mother, declared the new queen a witch and sentenced her to be burned to death at dawn the next day.

That night was the hardest night. Accused of a horrible crime, worried about her stolen baby, unable to speak to her beloved husband. So the girl did the only thing she could do. She tried to finish all the nettle shirts before

dawn, hoping that as she burned, her brothers would be safe.

But she failed. She didn't finish the shirts. When the sun rose and the guards came to take the girl outside, the last shirt only had one sleeve.

As the guards led her to the pile of branches in the center of the courtyard, the girl laid the shirts on the ground, one at each step, smoothed flat on the stones of the palace courtyard. But the twelfth shirt only had one sleeve.

Then she stepped to the pyre and let the guards tie her to the stake. She still didn't speak a word.

She looked at the old queen smiling and the young king weeping.

And she heard the sound of . . .

. . . wings beating.

As the guards lit the fire, she saw twelve beautiful white swans fly over the palace and land in the courtyard. As the flames warmed her feet and the smoke filled her silent throat, she saw the swans pick up the shirts and pull

 87

them over their feathery backs.

The swans grew tall and straight, the white feathers became black and brown and ginger and golden hair, and the pairs of wings became pairs of arms. But the last shirt only had one sleeve, so the last swan turned into a boy with one arm and one white wing.

Her twelve brothers stood in front of her as the flames grew higher and hotter and they shouted, "You can speak now, sister!"

So she called to her husband, "I didn't kill our baby; your mother stole our baby. The blood on my lips was hers."

The king looked at his mother and saw the truth in her face.

He dove forward and pulled his wife from the fire. Then he demanded that his mother take them to their stolen baby.

They found the baby in a pit in the forest, giggling and playing with the snakes and the toads. But when the old queen was thrown into the pit, the snakes didn't play with her.

The twelve brothers, their sister, and her new family all lived happily ever after (or as

happily as any group of people ever can).

But no matter how many nettles she spun and weaved and sewed into sleeves, the sister could never give her twelfth brother back his left arm. His one white wing was a reminder that, long ago, their mother had made a very silly wish.

The Wolf Arrow
Dutch Folktale

The soldier had fought his last battle for the king's army. He was returning home to his father's farm, where he hoped to settle to a more peaceful life.

He was an archer, skilled and strong. He still carried his bow but the quiver on his back only held one arrow, a souvenir of the life he was leaving behind. It was fletched with his favorite feathers, silvery gray feathers that made the arrow fly true.

He was nearing his home, walking softly along the country lane, when he heard singing. Not the loud chanting of an army singing to terrify the enemy or to cover up the fear in their own hearts but a cheerful melody in a light, high voice, singing a counting song about flowers.

He looked over the wall into the nearest field and saw a little girl sitting in the middle of a meadow, her head bent over a daisy chain as she sang her song.

The archer smiled. A world which contained daisies and singing children: this was why he was coming home.

Then he saw a dark shadow creeping through the grass and flowers. A low, long, hairy shadow, creeping toward the girl.

A wolf!

The wolf leaped.

The archer pulled his last arrow from his quiver, nocked it onto the string of his bow, drew the string back, and released the arrow. He didn't pause to aim because he knew his arrow would follow his eye.

As the arrow left the bow, the wolf was still leaping high in the air, aiming for the girl's neck.

The arrow struck the wolf in the shoulder. The wolf fell out of the air, howling in pain, and rolled over in the grass.

The archer jumped over the wall. The wolf ran off, limping.

The archer had no more arrows.

And the girl was screaming in shock. So he picked her up, carried her to the farmhouse at the end of the meadow, and put her in the arms of her mother.

Then he continued on his way home.

His family was delighted to see him. They prepared a feast to celebrate his return. "There haven't been so many lambs recently," said his father as they prepared the meat for roasting, "because we've been troubled by wolf attacks. There's one beast that takes children if they stray too far from home."

The archer mentioned, quietly, the wolf he had shot. His father patted his shoulder and said, "Yet another reason to celebrate."

The archer's mother invited all the neighbors, including the little girl's family, to the homecoming feast. Everyone in the district came, all but their next door neighbor from the farm down the track.

"Where's our next door neighbor?" the archer's mother wondered. "He normally has a great appetite for other people's food!" Everyone laughed and waited for the neighbor to show up.

But he never arrived, not when the smell of perfectly roasted meat wafted across the fields, not when the flames of the bonfire rose high in the sky, not when the singing got a bit too loud.

The archer and his father decided to check if their neighbor was alright. "It's not like him to miss a feast," said the archer's father as they crossed the fields.

When they reached the neighbor's house, the back door was wide open so the archer and his father walked in.

Their neighbor was lying on the stone floor of the kitchen. Stretched out, stiff, and cold,

with blood pooled under his chest and an arrow in his shoulder.

"That's my arrow," said the archer. "That's the arrow I shot at the wolf."

That's how they discovered their neighbor had feasted on stolen lambs and perhaps even stolen children.

The archer kept his one last arrow, not as a reminder of the wars he'd fought, but as a reminder that he had shot a werewolf and a warning that he could do it again.

For the rest of his long peaceful life, on his family's farm and on the farms around, the lambs grew fat all summer and the children played in safety.

And the wolf-gray arrow was never needed again.

Buzzard Boy
Mexican Folktale

O nce there was a boy who lived on a farm at the edge of the forest with his mom and dad.

One day, his dad said it was time for the boy to break ground and grow his own crops. His dad gave him an ax and his mom gave him a pile of warm tortillas and they said, "Go to the edge of the trees and clear a field for yourself. Cut down the trees, cut down the bushes, burn the scrub, then you can

plant these seeds and grow yourself a field of corn."

The boy walked toward the forest. When he reached the best place for a field, he lifted the ax and swung it at a tree.

Thunk. The ax hit the trunk. "Ouch! That was sore on my hands."

Thunk, again. "Ouch!"

Thunk, one more time. His hands were stinging and the tree still hadn't fallen over.

The boy sighed. This was going to be hard work and he didn't feel like hard work. So he left the ax sticking out of the tree, sat down at the edge of the forest, and ate one of his tortillas.

Then he lay down and gazed up past the trees at the cool blue sky.

He saw birds flying above him. "Birds don't have to work," he muttered. "They're free to fly about all day and go wherever they want."

He saw a big bird circle above him.

"Oi! Buzzard! You don't know how lucky you are, up there with no work to do! I wish we could swap."

The buzzard circled lower.

"Oi? Buzzard? Do you want to swap? You come down here and be a boy, and I'll go up there and be a buzzard, free as the air."

The buzzard circled even lower.

"Come on, buzzard. It'll be fun! Swap your feathers for my clothes and eat my mom's warm tortillas for lunch."

The buzzard landed beside him. The big black and red bird looked at the ax, at the tortillas, and at the boy.

The buzzard nodded. "Let's swap."

The buzzard pulled off his feathers and the boy pulled off his shirt, and they swapped.

The boy's nose became a beak; the buzzard's claws became toes. Soon the boy who was now a buzzard was testing out his wide wings, and the buzzard who was now a boy was wrapping his fingers around the ax handle.

"Thanks!" said the brand new buzzard and flapped his wings to fly off.

"Hold on!" said the brand new boy. "Tell me how to be a boy."

"You've been watching me; just do what I did."

"But all you've done this morning is lie around and eat. There must be more to being a boy than that."

"If you really want to work like a farm boy, chop down some trees and bushes, burn the scrub, then plant seeds." The brand new buzzard flapped up into the air.

The brand new boy called after him, "Don't you want to know how to be a buzzard?"

"How hard can it be?" The brand new buzzard laughed as he flew away.

The brand new boy pulled the ax out of the tree and swung it, enjoying the strange new strength of his arms and legs and the heavy solidity of his new body.

He cut down a dozen trees, ate tortillas for lunch, then cut down another dozen trees. As he piled them, the farmer arrived and said, "That's an excellent day's work, son. Come home for your tea."

So the brand new boy followed the farmer to the farmhouse for a hot meal, then lay in a

soft bed all night, listening to rain on the roof.

He returned to the edge of the forest the next day to continue clearing his own field. As he chopped at the first tree of the day, the brand new buzzard flew down and asked, "How do buzzards stay warm and dry?"

"Buzzards don't. Birds live outside, so buzzards are cold at night and wet in the rain."

"Ah. And who gives a buzzard his meals?"

"No one. You have to find your own food. That's why I accepted your offer to swap; now I sleep with a roof over my head and I eat your mother's lovely cooking."

"You might have a roof and tortillas but I can fly free above the forest." The brand new buzzard flew off, while the brand new boy chopped down trees.

The next day, as the brand new boy started cutting down bushes, the brand new buzzard flapped into the clearing, looking a bit scrawny. "How do I find my own food? I tried to hunt rabbits but they're too fast. I tried to eat berries but my beak's too big."

The brand new boy put down his ax

and stretched his arms. Then he handed the brand new buzzard half a tortilla and said, "Buzzards don't hunt fresh meat or eat fresh fruit. Buzzards scavenge dead things. Buzzards eat corpses."

"Yuck!" said the brand new buzzard. After a pause, he added, "I know that should be yuck but actually my tummy is rumbling at the thought. How do I find a nice, juicy corpse?"

"You have to hunt for gases rising like smoke from a body as it cools, then follow the fumes down." The brand new boy picked up the ax again. "I used to like the smell of cooling corpses, but now I prefer the smell of baking tortillas."

The brand new boy cut down another bush and the brand new buzzard flew off to find and follow fumes.

That afternoon, as the brand new boy piled scrubby bits of bush around the field to burn it to the ground, the brand new buzzard tried to find fumes that would lead him to food.

First he dive-bombed a kettle as a traveler made coffee, then he got his talons caught in

a girl's hair when she went to a party wearing too much perfume, then he nearly landed on a fresh, steaming cow pie.

Finally he found a hot pillar of intriguing fumes and he thought, "That's it!" He dove down through the whirling warmth.

He dove right into the heart of the fire that the brand new boy had lit to clear the field.

The brand new buzzard dove into the center of the flames. And he couldn't get out. His feathers were smoldering, his eyes were watering, he couldn't work out which way was up or down.

The brand new buzzard was burning.

Then two hands, blistered with hard work, dragged him out. The brand new boy pulled the brand new buzzard out of the fire.

The brand new boy said, "Do you want to swap again? I like being a farmer, and I like living in a house and eating tortillas. But if

you want to swap again, if it's too hard to be a buzzard, I will give you back your clothes and your job."

As the brand new buzzard preened his singed feathers, he looked at the hoe, the rake, and the sacks of seeds at the edge of the new field. "Being a boy is too much work. I like being a buzzard, with the freedom of the sky. It's not easy but I will learn to be the best buzzard I can be."

The buzzard flew away.

The boy cleared the rest of the field, planted the seeds, harvested his crop, and eventually ate tortillas made from his own corn.

The boy never spoke to the buzzard again. But he often saw him, circling above the farm. The boy waved his arms and the buzzard dipped his wings then danced in the air, being the best buzzard he could be.

Many years later, when his own children, his own boys and girls, looked up at the blue sky and said, "Wouldn't it be wonderful to be free as a bird?" the farmer who used to be a buzzard smiled. "It's not easy being a bird.

I wouldn't swap it for a watertight house, a pile of warm tortillas, and a bit of hard work. I wouldn't swap it at all."

The Laidly Wyrm
Northumbrian legend

Above the long, golden beach at Bamburgh, a castle stands proud on a hill.

Once upon a time, the king of Northumbria lived in that castle. He had a queen and two children: a boy called Wynne and a girl called Margaret. The two children played together in the castle and on the beach, the little sister often annoying her big brother by dancing around him, getting in his way, giggling and

smiling and being hard to dislike however irritating she was.

The king's children grew up happy. Soon Wynne was old enough to learn how to be a king. He decided the best way to learn was to go on a quest with a ship, a crew, and a long, sharp sword to defeat as many monsters as he could.

On the day he left, his little sister didn't annoy him at all. She just kissed him on the cheek, wished him an exciting quest, and said good-bye.

The king continued to rule Northumbria with the queen's help, and Margaret learned to play on her own.

One winter, the queen died. The king was left with only Margaret to help him. She had to grow up fast. She became her father's advisor, wise and kind. She took control of the keys of the castle: the keys to every chamber and the keys to all the treasure.

One spring, the king went hunting in the forest, where he met the most beautiful woman he had ever seen. He fell instantly in love and married her on the spot.

They rode back to the castle, the king smiling because he thought he'd found someone wonderful to share his life with, the new queen smiling because she thought she'd soon have complete power over the king, the castle, the kingdom, and the treasure.

Then she saw the slim figure of Margaret, waiting on the steps of the castle. As they rode closer, the new queen saw Margaret's cheerful, clever face and the heavy bunch of keys on her belt. The new queen realized she would never have complete power over the king or the kingdom while Margaret was by the king's side.

So the new queen decided to get rid of Margaret.

She took a few days to gather what she needed, then one night she crept down to the basement to cast a spell.

From her left pocket, she took a long white bone. "The rib of a dragon," she whispered. From her right pocket, she took a long dark hair. "The hair of the daughter," she whispered.

She knotted the hair around the bone and circled the palm of her hand over it nine times. As she passed her hand over the bone, she thought about how to make this the strongest spell ever.

Every spell has a weakness and it's wise for the spellmaker to choose what its weakness will be. To make her spell strong, the new queen chose the most unlikely way to break it.

"You will stay in the loathsome form I give you, annoying child, until you are kissed, not by a lover or a friend, but by a boy who is far overseas learning to kill your kind. You will stay in this shape until you are kissed by the king's son, Wynne!"

The new queen snapped her fingers. And upstairs in her bedroom, Margaret turned into a . . .

. . . dragon!

Margaret didn't know she'd become a dragon, of course, because she was asleep. She found out early the next morning when her maid came in to help her brush her hair.

The maid saw a huge, green serpent coiled on the bed and she screamed.

Margaret woke, sat up, looked at herself, and saw her green scales. She screamed too. But she didn't have the right throat for a scream any more, so the scream came out as a roar.

The maid screamed, the dragon roared, and the castle shook.

Margaret slid out of the window, slithered down the castle wall, and hid in the darkest hole she could find. She didn't want to be a dragon. She didn't want anyone to see her.

But she grew hungry, so after a week of hiding, she crept out to search for food.

She tried to catch a sheep but when she chased the flock, the shepherd ran off, shouting, "Dragon! That dragon wants to eat me!" But the dragon didn't eat him, the dragon ate a sheep.

She tried to catch a goat but

when she chased the flock, the goatherd ran off, shouting, "Dragon! That dragon wants to eat me!" But the dragon didn't eat him, the dragon ate a goat.

She tried to catch a cow but when she chased the herd, the farmer ran off, shouting, "Dragon! That dragon wants to eat me!" But the dragon didn't eat him, the dragon ate a cow.

The people ran to the castle and demanded to see the king. "Help us, your majesty! There's a dragon trying to eat us! Please kill the dragon for us!"

The new queen was about to say, "Yes, let's kill the dragon," when the king asked, "A dragon, trying to eat you? Really? How many people has it eaten?"

"Erm . . . none. No people at all actually . . ."

"So what has it eaten?"

"Sheep. Goats. Cows." They told the king exactly what had happened.

And the king, who was a wise king in most matters, even when he was distracted by his new queen and his missing daughter, said, "If

it had wanted to eat you, you'd be chewed up and swallowed by now. It's not a dangerous dragon, just a hungry one. If you feed it every day, it will leave you alone."

So the dragon coiled around a tall rock called Spindleston Heugh, and the bravest of the local people delivered a big bucket of milk and a dozen large loaves to the foot of the rock every day. The dragon was full, the people were safe, and so were the sheep and goats and cows.

But the people weren't happy. They didn't like having a great, long serpent of a dragon wound around a rock so close by, with its bright green scales, long white teeth, and sad eyes watching them as they farmed and fished. The locals called the dragon the Laidly Wyrm, or loathsome worm, and went on long detours so they didn't have to walk too close to it.

After a few weeks of dragon-feeding and dragon-avoidance, they went back to the king and said, "It may not be hungry but we still don't feel safe with a dragon coiled around

a rock so close to our homes and the castle. We'd still like you to kill it."

The king nodded. "The best person to rid us of a dragon is the boy who went off to learn to kill them. I miss having my children around me since Margaret vanished, so I shall summon young Wynne home again."

A short message was sent: "Wynne, come home urgently." Soon Wynne, who had killed almost enough dragons, manticores, and basilisks to feel qualified to be a king, started the journey back to Bamburgh.

The new queen was furious. She'd just got rid of the daughter, now here was the son heading home. She had to get rid of him too so she would be the only one with influence over the king.

Late one night, she crept to the basement and conjured up ninety-nine spiky black imps. She gave each of them a bowl of water and a fishbone spoon and ordered them to stir up a storm.

As each of the ninety-nine imps stirred, the water began to swirl and splash, and the

water in the basement called to the water in the sea.

The water near the castle shivered and swirled. Waves reached up to grab air, then smashed down and shattered. The breezes near the castle shifted and whirled and became winds which surged and howled.

The imps were stirring in different directions and at different speeds, so the waves and winds were arriving from all angles, crashing into each other, battling and building a massive storm at sea.

The magical storm roared around Wynne's ship as he approached home. But it didn't sink him. While he'd been away, Wynne had learned to kill monsters and he'd also learned to keep himself safe from dark magic, so he was returning in a ship of rowan wood, the only tree that resists magic.

Wynne's ship floated calmly on the top of the soaring waves and drove a straight line through the gusting winds.

The new queen screamed in frustration. She kicked over the imps' bowls and yelled, "Hide

yourselves on the beach and when that boy comes ashore, tear him to pieces!"

The imps scuttled down to the beach, buried themselves in the sand, and waited for Wynne to land.

But when the ship approached the beach, there was a sudden splash as the dragon leaped from her rock and landed in the water between the ship and the shore.

The dragon flicked at the ship with her tail, the dragon danced in the waves, the dragon coiled around the ship, and the dragon made it impossible for the ship to land.

Wynne said, "What an annoying creature." He and his men tried to kill the dragon with arrows and spears. But her scales were too thick and she was moving too fast. The dragon kept dancing and coiling and generally making a nuisance of herself so the ship couldn't land on the long, golden beach.

The golden beach that was hiding ninety-nine imps . . .

Eventually, Wynne said, "This irritating dragon won't let us land here, so let's try the bay to the north."

As soon as the ship turned away from the beach below the castle, the dragon stopped bothering the sailors and coiled back around her rock.

Once Wynne had landed safely, he said to his men, "Before I go to the castle to greet my father, I must deal with that annoying green wyrm." He drew his long sword, now tempered with the hot blood of dozens of monsters, and he strode up to Spindleston Heugh.

The dragon was coiled around the rock with her tail at the top and her head at the bottom. She hung there, upside down, and watched Wynne approach. Wynne stepped right up to the rock and stared at the dragon's throat, searching for a soft patch he could pierce with his sword.

The dragon tipped her head to one side and smiled.

Wynne thought, "That's unusual. I've killed

many dragons, and not one of them has smiled at me just before I attack."

He looked at the dragon, hanging upside down, with its head on one side, smiling at him. He thought of the dragon dancing and bouncing in the waves and annoying him by getting in his way.

He said, "How strange, dragon; you remind me of my little sister."

The dragon grinned even wider.

He lowered his sword. "I can't kill something that reminds me of my little sister."

He laid his sword on the ground.

The dragon's head darted forward and kissed Wynne on the cheek.

Wynne laughed. "What a friendly dragon. I suppose one kiss deserves another." He leaned forward and kissed the dragon on her scaly green snout.

The dragon changed into his little sister, Margaret.

She landed in a heap at the bottom of the rock. Wynne helped her up and wrapped her in his cloak.

"Margaret! Who did this to you? Who turned you into a wyrm?"

"The new queen who replaced our mother."

"Then I will go and finish her, the way I nearly finished you." He picked up his sword.

Margaret said, "No, there are better ways to deal with her."

She led him along the shore toward the castle. As they passed his ship, still seaworthy but a bit battered by the whirling water and the dancing dragon, Margaret pried off a splinter of rowan wood.

When they reached the castle, the new queen was trying to leave with as much silk and treasure as she could carry. Margaret tapped the new queen over the heart with the rowan wood, and the new queen returned to her true form. A toad. A squat, warty, damp-looking toad.

The toad hopped off with no treasure at all, leaving Margaret and Wynne to enter the castle to meet their father, then live happily and wisely for many years.

And that is why Spindleston Heugh still bears the marks of a serpent's scales coiling around it, and why you can sometimes hear a toad croak in the grounds of Bamburgh Castle. But don't worry; you'll be quite safe if you carry a bit of rowan wood with you . . .

The Accidental Wolf Cub
German Folktale

There are many ways to become a werewolf. Being bitten by a wolf. Drinking water from a wolf's footprint. Or wearing a wolfskin belt . . .

Once upon a time there was a little boy who wanted to play with a wolfskin belt.

He could see the wolfskin belt hanging on the back of the door in his house.

The belt was hairy, gray, old, worn. Not like everything else in the house, which his mom

kept clean and polished and mended. But his mom never touched the wolfskin belt. Neither did his big sister, nor his granny.

No one but his dad touched the wolfskin belt. Even his dad only touched it as the sun went down and the moon rose, a couple of nights a month. He would unhook it from the nail on the door and, as he wrapped it around his waist, he would smile goodbye to his family, then leave the house before he'd finished buckling the belt.

There was always fresh meat on the table the next day.

The little boy wanted to play with the belt.

He had plenty of other things to play with. Wooden sheep and cows and ducks carved by his father. Tin soldiers from a box his granny gave him. A patchwork cloak made from scraps by his mom so he could be a brave knight or a traveling musician.

But these toys never seemed as much fun as the toys just out of reach. So he wanted to play with that wolfskin belt.

One day, when his mom and big sister were

in the garden digging carrots, his dad was in the fields, and his granny was dozing by the fire, her knitting on her knee, the little boy built a tower.

He built a tower from a chair, a stool, and his mom's sewing box, then he climbed to the top and reached for the belt.

CRASH! The tower collapsed.

His granny said, "What? Humph." And started to snore again.

He built the tower again. The chair. The stool. The sewing box. He pushed the tower against the door to keep it steady. He climbed to the top, he reached for the belt, and he touched it.

CRASH! The tower collapsed.

His granny said, "Who? Humph." And started to snore again.

The little boy lay on the floor surrounded by spools of thread and scraps of material, but he had the wolfskin belt in his hands.

He wrapped it around his tummy. He was going to be his dad. He was going to be a big tall man and do big tall man things.

He stood up tall and buckled the belt around his tummy.

Suddenly the little boy felt tingly all over. He sneezed and scratched.

Then his feet scrabbled on the newly slippy floor and he fell down.

He tried to stand. But his feet and hands were strange and awkward, so he fell over again.

He shook his head, waggling his ears, and tried to stand again. He got onto his hands and knees. Then he stood on his legs and tried to walk toward his granny.

But his hind legs couldn't hold his weight. He lost his balance. He tumbled down onto the rag rug on the floor. His toenails got caught in the rug and he got all tangled up, wrapping the rug around himself. He wriggled and scrambled and crawled out on the smooth wooden floor.

Crawling was easier than walking, so he tried that, slipping and sliding with those nails clicking. At first he tumbled and rolled around the floor. But finally he learned how to move on all fours.

He bounced and jumped and leaped around the floor.

He grinned. This was fun.

Then he noticed the tail. There was a tail! Just out of reach. A long, waggly, furry silver tail. A tail! What a great toy.

He grabbed for the tail with his hands but his fingers didn't seem to be doing anything useful.

So he grabbed the tail with his teeth.

OUCH! That hurt, and the tail flicked away. Temptingly.

He grabbed for the tail again and it flicked away again. He chased the tail round and round in a circle until he was dizzy and fell down on the rug again.

But chasing the tail had been fun. And fast. Now he wanted to see how fast he could move on all fours. He started slow at first, then got faster and faster, running and springing under the table and around the chairs and jumping his full length over the rug.

Now he was controlling all four legs but he kept forgetting that tail.

The tail knocked over the jug of milk cooling on the shelf by the door and his granny's cup of tea. The house was filled with the splash of milk and the crash of china, and his granny woke up.

"What? Who's there? What's going on?"

His granny sounded worried, so he bounced over to give her a cuddle.

She screamed. "*Wolf!*"

He looked around. Wolf? Where was the wolf? He would protect his granny from the wolf! He snuggled up to his granny's legs. She screamed again and whacked him with her knitting.

His mom and sister ran into the house, and his sister yelled, "Where's my little brother? That wolf has eaten him!"

His granny shouted, "Cut it open! Cut open its belly in case it swallowed him whole. That works in fairy tales!"

"No!" said the mom, "No! I wonder . . . ? Don't hurt the cub. We'll try to catch it." She

said to his sister, "Fetch your father, but shut the door on your way out."

The little boy watched as his mom grabbed a blanket and threw it toward him. A game!

The little boy bounced off, tail waving, paws skidding, racing around the kitchen in a glorious game of chase, howling with laughter as his mom and his granny tried to stop him. They threw shawls and tablecloths over him to try to wrap him and catch him. Between them, they knocked over every chair and jug and bowl and stool and even his box of tin soldiers, all clattering onto the floor.

Finally his mom threw the little boy's own patchwork cloak at his feet. His claws caught in it, and he tripped and tumbled to the floor.

His mom wrapped him in his dress-up costume and said, "Hush, hush, hush."

His dad walked in the door and said calmly, "Oh dear."

His dad took the wolf cub from his mom's arms. He unwrapped the cloak, scratched the cub's furry chin, and smiled. Then he ran his hand along the wolf's tummy

and pulled off the wolfskin belt.

And there in his arms was the little boy, all soft skin and fingers again. The little boy grinned and giggled. "That was fun, Daddy. Can I do it again?"

"No!" said his mom. "Never again!"

"Not yet," said his dad, "not yet." Then he whispered in his son's ear, "But you'll make a fine wolf when you grow up . . ."

How to Track Down Shape-Shifters

Shape-shifting seems like a wonderful magical power. Have you ever imagined being a bird, or a wolf, or a dragon? Have you ever imagined flying or running on four legs? Shape-shifting does seem fantastic, if you can control it.

But if a change of shape is forced on you, if you've been cursed or enchanted to become a swan or a frog or a snake, it could be terrifying! (As well as very inconvenient.)

Shape-shifting was one of the first kinds of magic I heard about as a child because there are lots of shape-shifters in Scottish legends and folktales. So I use images and magic from shape-shifting legends in my adventure novels. And I'm always on the lookout for shape-shifters I've never met before.

There are shape-shifting stories in almost every culture, and most shape-shifter stories

are wonderful: vivid and exciting, with lots of sharp teeth and dark magic. So it's been difficult choosing which stories to include in this book. I've tried to include lots of different kinds of animals, in stories from lots of different parts of the world.

In myth, legend, and folklore, it's not just the characters who change shape. The stories themselves can change shape too. I believe that all oral stories, stories told and heard and remembered and told again, change as they pass from teller to audience to teller.

I've altered all these stories as I tell them to make them work for me and for the audience I'm telling to. And if you tell them, I hope you'll change them a little bit too!

I'm very grateful to the storytellers, collectors, and writers (many of whom are listed in the sources below) who inspired me and this collection. I hope you're inspired to track down more shape-shifter stories, or even make up your own. What animal would you like to become, just for a little while?

The Snake Prince
Punjabi Folktale

It's quite common for people in folklore and fairy tales to marry snakes accidentally, and this is my favorite version of that widespread story, because I really like the snake becoming a necklace, then becoming a baby. This tale was told to a Major Campbell in the Punjab, then published in Andrew Lang's *The Olive Fairy Book* (Longmans, Green and Co., 1907). The princess in Lang's version is a bit inclined to weeping and fainting, so she has more backbone in my retelling.

The First Werewolves
Greek myth

This is one of many stories from Greek mythology about shape-shifters. I first came across it in Ovid's *Metamorphoses* (Penguin Classics, 2004; originally published around 8 AD), which is a great source for stories of unfortunate people turned into plants and animals when they fall foul of the gods. (Though Lycaon deserved it more than most!) Ovid tells the story about Jove because it's a Roman version of the older Greek myth. The nasty detail that Lycaon cooked his own son comes from Robert Graves's *Greek Myths* (Penguin, 1955). In many versions, it's this bowl of boy stew which leads to the gods' anger and the great flood, but that's a different story!

Catching Loki
Norse myth

I often tell the story of how Loki tricked Hodur, the god of winter, into killing his brother Baldur, the god of summer (you can find my retelling in *Winter's Tales*, A&C Black, 2013). And sometimes, if the audience want to know what happened next, I tell the story of how Loki was caught by his own cleverness. I found Loki's house with four doors in *Teutonic Myth and Legend* by Donald A Mackenzie (The Gresham Publishing Company, 1912).

The Ashkelon Witches
Jewish Folktale

I loved this story the moment I found it
in Howard Schwartz's book *Elijah's Violin*
(Oxford University Press, 1983). I love the
clever way the rabbi defeats the witches
with the rain and the way the witches are all
transformed into something appropriate at the
end. In this retelling, the idea of a baby being
turned into a caterpillar rather than a butterfly
isn't mine—my younger daughter suggested it
when I was telling her the story on a bus.

Turnskin
Breton Folktale

I first caught sight of this tale when I was researching a novel about werewolves and finally tracked it down to *The Lais of Marie de France* (Penguin Classics, 1986). I've told this story many times, and like most of the stories I work with, it has changed as I tell it, often in response to queries and questions from the audience. The particular ending I've used in this collection is one suggested by P5 pupils at Trinity Primary School in Edinburgh. Thanks for sharing your ideas!

The Swallow's Search
Egyptian myth

The story of Isis and her lost husband Osiris has been told in many ways for many thousands of years. I first read it in *Tales of Ancient Egypt* by Roger Lancelyn Green (published by The Bodley Head, 1967) when I was a child (not quite thousands of years ago!). I've come across many versions since but images from the first one I read are still burning bright in my head.

The Frog, the Flies, and the Frying Pan
Scottish Folktale

I love having fun with this version of the Frog Prince, where the curse is lifted not by a kiss but by a whack on the head! There are various versions of it, but I first found it in *Scottish Folk and Fairy Tales* (Penguin Popular Classics, 1992), retold by Elizabeth Grierson. I'll admit that I've changed the end a little, because marrying a handsome prince isn't everyone's idea of a happy ending!

Fooled by Foxes
Japanese Folktale

This story was inspired by a kitsune tale in *Tales of Old Japan* by Baron Algernon Bertram Freeman-Mitford (Macmillan, 1871). I realized when I reread the source (having told the story many times since I first read it) that I've retained the central idea of a young man claiming he won't be fooled by foxes but I've changed a few of the details, particularly how badly the first fox is injured.

Ceridwen's Potion
Welsh legend

I love Ceridwen's power but also her cruelty.
The heroines in stories aren't always nice
people! My main source for this retelling is the
wonderful *Encyclopedia of Goddesses and
Heroines* by Patricia Monaghan (Greenwood
Press, 2010). The shape-shifting chase scene is
very similar to a chase in one of my favorite
Scottish stories (The King of the Black Art)
but Gwion's story ends very differently.

The Gold Sea
Canadian tribal tale

This is my retelling of a story from *Legends of Vancouver* by E. Pauline Johnson-Tekahionwake (Quarry Press, 1991; originally published by Saturday Sunset Presses, 1911), which is one of my most treasured collections of ancient tales. I hope I've managed to stay true to the spirit and flavor of the tale, but as I've told it I've made a few changes to tell it in my voice. It's definitely the most humane monster-killing story I've ever found.

The Swan Brothers
Norwegian Folktale

The brothers turned into birds is a story that appears in lots of cultures with lots of variations, many of which have inspired elements of this retelling. It's hard to name a country and credit a source (there are similar Danish stories and German ones and Irish ones) but my retelling here is probably inspired most by the wild ducks story in *Tales From the Norse* by George Webbe Dasent (Blackie and Son, 1906).

The Wolf Arrow
Dutch Folktale

I found this old tale in the amazing (though very dark and seriously weird) *Book of Werewolves* by the Reverend Sabine Baring-Gould (Dover Publications Inc., 2006; originally published by Smith, Elder & Co. in 1865). The story of a neighbor being identified as a werewolf because of a wound inflicted on a wolf is very common but I chose to include this one because I liked the archer recognizing his own arrow. As always I changed a few details as I told the story and when I reread the source I was surprised to discover that he wasn't a soldier in the original because he is so clearly a soldier in my head!

Buzzard Boy
Mexican Folktale

This is my retelling of a Tzotzil Mayan tale from *Latin American Folktales* by John Bierhorst (Pantheon Books, 2002), and it may be the story that I've changed most as I've worked with it, mainly because I first told it to an audience of young children and it seemed natural to change the main character from a lazy man into a lazy boy. Now that the reckless boy who swaps places with the buzzard is a living character in my head, I can't swap him back to an unknown workshy husband!

The Laidly Wyrm
Northumbrian legend

My granny was from Northumberland, and one of my favorite places in the north of England is the beach below Bamburgh Castle. So I love this story of magic and monsters, set in that beautiful and dramatic place. I first read about the Laidly Wyrm when I was very young, in Roger Lancelyn Green's *A Book Of Dragons*, retold by Joseph Jacobs (Puffin Books, 1970).

The Accidental Wolf Cub
German Folktale

Another story inspired by the *Book of Werewolves* by Sabine Baring-Gould. I read his very short version of this old tale, then started describing the story to my own children, and the characters just came to life as I talked about them. So this is my own imagining of what might happen if a little boy accidentally became a werewolf cub.